HEALTH AND HYGIENE

LIFE GUIDES

HEALTH AND HYGIENE

Brian R. Ward

Series consultant:
Dr Alan Maryon-Davis
MB, BChir, MSc, MRCP, FFCM

Franklin Watts
London · New York · Toronto · Sydney

© 1988 Franklin Watts

First published in 1988 by
Franklin Watts
12a Golden Square
London W1

First published in the USA by
Franklin Watts Inc.
387 Park Avenue South
New York, N.Y. 10016

First published in Australia by
Franklin Watts Australia
14 Mars Road
Lane Cove
New South Wales 2066

UK ISBN: 0 86313 666 4
US ISBN: 0-531-10561-X
Library of Congress Catalog Card No: 87-51698

Design: Howard Dyke

Picture research: Anne-Marie Ehrlich

Illustrations: Andrew Aloof, John Bavosi, Dick Bonson, Chapman Bounford, Howard Dyke, Sally Launder

Photographs:
Ardea 21*tl*
Charing Cross Hospital Medical School 15(*6*), 26
CNER 21*c*
Sally and Richard Greenhill 7, 39*t*
Hutchinson Library 41*t*
Science Photo Library 11, 25, 31, 43
Tropix 7
John Watney 9 (*4*), 15(*1–4*), 23, 28, 39*b*
James Webb 9(*1–3, 5–7*), 15(*5*), 17, 21*tr*, 30, 41*b*, 42
Zefa 10, 29

Printed in Belgium

Contents

Introduction	6
Life on our bodies	8
The spread of infection	10
Personal hygiene	12
Minor infections	14
Parasite diseases	16
Food hygiene	18
Pests that spread disease	20
Vacation precautions	22
Coughs and sneezes	24
Sore throats	26
Measles and rubella	28
Chickenpox and mumps	30
The common infections	32
Fighting disease	34
Developing immunity against disease	36
Protection against disease	38
Fighting disease with drugs	40
Tropical diseases	42
AIDS: a new threat to health	44
Glossary	46
Index	48

Introduction

What is hygiene? And why is it important? Hygiene is simply a way of protecting ourselves from the billions of microscopic organisms which surround us, and sometimes cause illness.

Hygiene is an important way of preventing some forms of disease. It can mean simply washing your hands after using the toilet, for example, or cleaning your teeth thoroughly. But there are many other ways in which hygiene is important for disease prevention. The water we drink has been purified to remove harmful organisms, and many foods are specially treated to control organisms that can cause infection. Proper attention to hygiene in the way we live and work has helped to control many diseases which, only a few generations ago, killed millions of people, especially children, every year.

Many diseases caused by infection can be prevented by **vaccination**. You were probably given vaccines by injection when you were very young to protect you from unpleasant or serious childhood infections. Diseases that cannot be prevented in this way must be controlled with drugs.

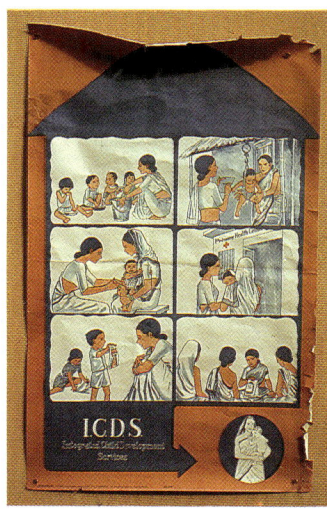

Health education is especially important in third world countries to help people understand how disease is spread. Posters such as this encourage mothers to bring their babies to health clinics for check-ups and vaccination.

Opposite
Babies and young children are vaccinated to protect them from infections. The use of vaccines has wiped out diseases such as smallpox that once claimed many lives.

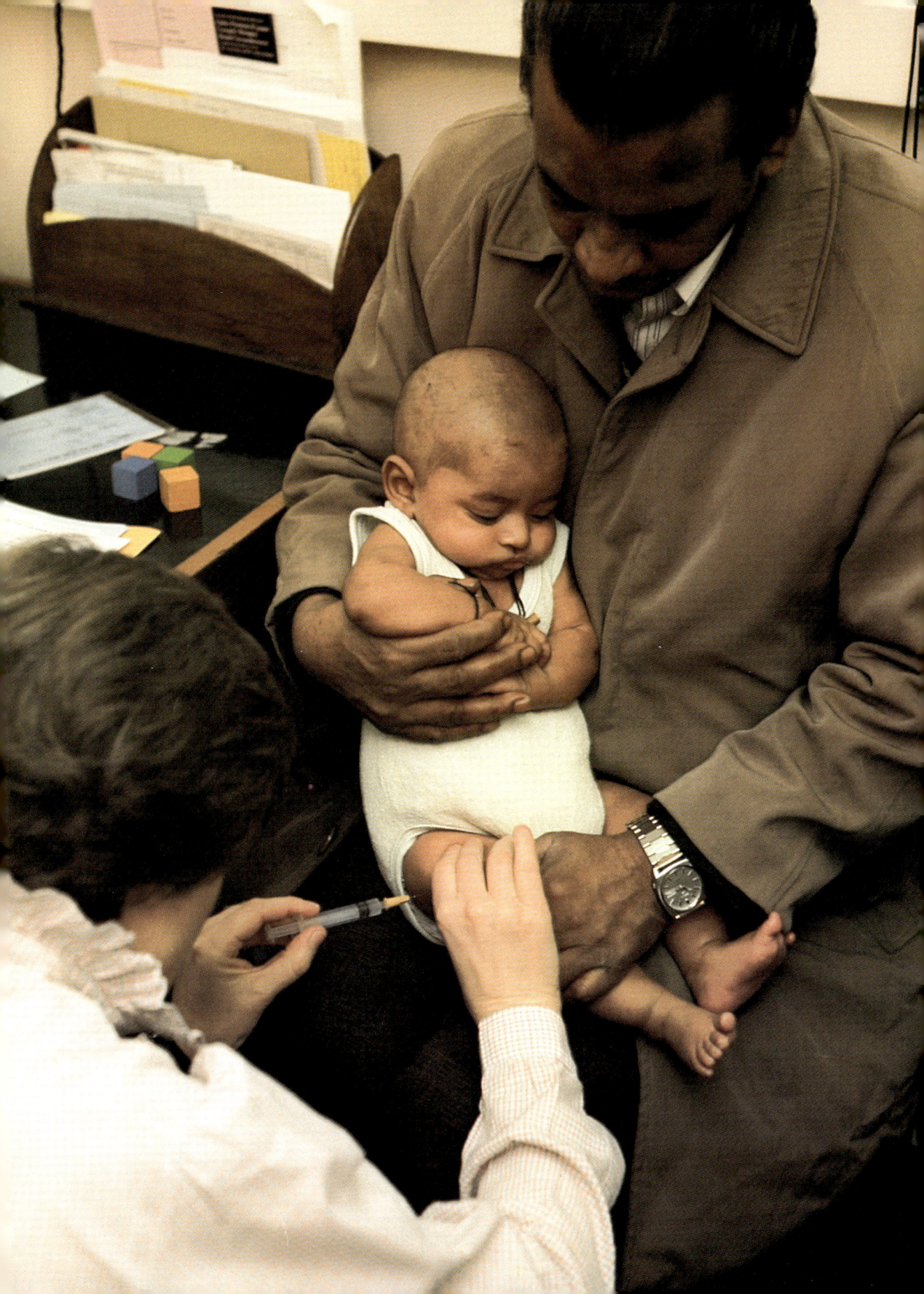

Life on our bodies

Viruses are tiny organisms that can damage cells and cause disease if they enter the body.

1 Virus becomes attached to a living cell in the body.
2 Virus passes into the cell, shedding its outer coating.
3 Virus takes over the function of the cell.
4 Cell is turned into a "factory" producing more viruses.
5 New virus particles escape, damaging the cell.

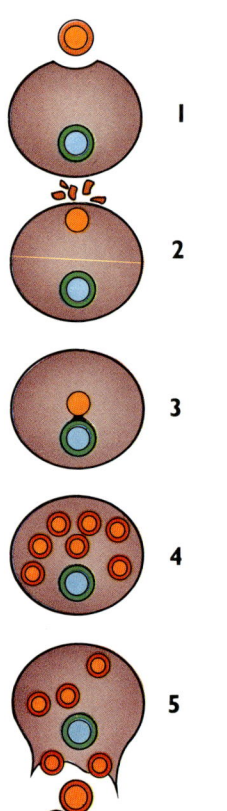

The whole surface of your body is covered with huge quantities of microscopic organisms. Even more live inside your body. Most of these are harmless and actually have a useful function. Organisms that live in the digestive system help to break down and digest food. But other types of organism can cause disease.

Bacteria, **viruses**, **yeasts** and **fungi** can all threaten health. Bacteria are very small, simple forms of life which can grow very quickly under the right conditions. Once they get into the body they reproduce and multiply. Some bacteria attack the tissues directly. Others produce substances, called **toxins**, which are extremely poisonous. The body reacts strongly against these invaders, and this may make us ill.

Viruses are another very common type of disease organism. They are even smaller and simpler than bacteria. Outside the body a virus is a helpless particle, but if it enters the body it will invade a living cell and multiply freely. Once inside the cell, it takes over the cell's life processes, damaging or destroying it.

Each type of bacterium or virus usually attacks a particular part of the body. However, sometimes the organisms, or substances produced by them, are carried in the blood.

Meningitis is a serious inflammation of the thin layer of tissue covering the brain. It may be caused by viruses or by tiny round bacteria called **cocci**.

Some of the most severe throat infections are caused by streptococci, tiny bacteria that cause a high temperature and sore throat.

Tuberculosis or TB is a disease starting in the lungs, caused by bacteria. It usually progresses slowly, and can be completely prevented by a simple vaccination.

Pneumonia is an inflammation of the lungs caused by various types of bacteria or viruses. It usually attacks people who are weakened by other illnesses.

Hepatitis A is a liver disease caused by a virus. It damages the liver and causes the skin and whites of the eyes to become jaundiced, or yellow-colored.

Staphylococcus is a type of bacterium that can cause boils and **abscesses**. This organism lives on the skin, and can invade the body through the hair **follicles**.

Cystitis is a bladder infection which is often caused by bacteria. It makes it very painful to urinate, and the infection often recurs after several weeks.

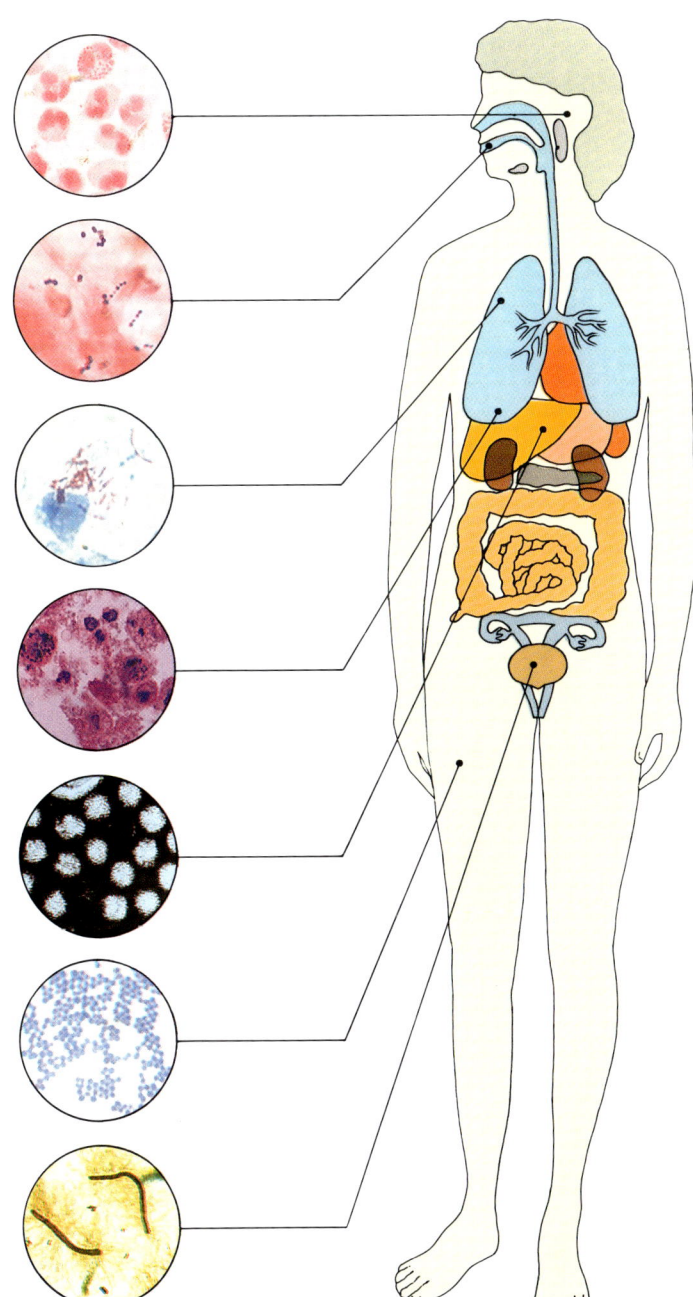

The spread of infection

There are several ways in which illness can be spread. Sometimes you can catch an illness by being in contact with a sick person. Diseases that are spread in this way are said to be **contagious**, and they spread very quickly, especially among groups of children playing together.

Infectious illnesses are often spread by coughs and sneezes. Tiny droplets of water are sprayed through the air, carrying with them bacteria or viruses from the mouth and nose. If you breathe in some of these droplets, you may

Commuters traveling in crowded trains or buses are exposed to bacteria and viruses coughed and sneezed out by people who are already infected. This is often how infections such as colds and flu are spread.

become infected. This is why it is important to cover the nose and mouth with a tissue or handkerchief when sneezing or coughing, to prevent germs from being spread.

Some organisms that cause very serious diseases are spread between users of illegal drugs who share the same needle, passing on contaminated blood.

Insects spread many diseases by transferring infectious material to our food or water. Biting insects can also pick up bacteria or viruses from the blood of an infected person and pass them on to other people.

When you sneeze, microscopic water droplets are sprayed into the air. If you have a cold, these droplets are laden with bacteria and viruses. And if these droplets are inhaled by other people, they may catch the infection.

Personal hygiene

The microscopic life that swarms on the skin is not usually dangerous, but it can cause problems if you do not pay attention to personal hygiene. Bacteria feed on oily substances present in perspiration, and in doing so they can produce unpleasant smells. This is particularly noticeable in the parts of the body which perspire most, like the armpits, groin and feet, unless they are washed thoroughly and frequently.

You can buy many aids to personal hygiene in any drugstore or supermarket. For care of the teeth, you can buy floss and mouthwashes as well as toothpaste. And there are many types of medicated soap, shampoos and skin-care products.

Because your hands come into contact with disease organisms which can then get into your food, it is very important to keep your hands clean. Wash your hands thoroughly with soap and water before eating and after going to the bathroom.

Dirt beneath the fingernails can contain huge numbers of bacteria, which can easily be transferred to the mouth and cause disease. Keep nails trimmed and use a nailbrush to remove every trace of dirt.

Gum inflammation and tooth decay, as well as bad breath, can be avoided if the teeth are cleaned properly, morning and night. It is important to clean every surface of the teeth thoroughly to remove **plaque** from the crevices between the teeth. Your dentist will advise you how to clean your teeth effectively.

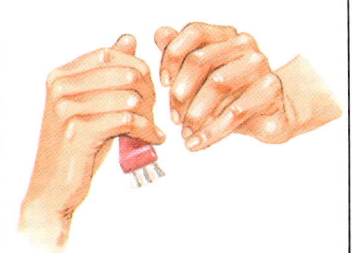
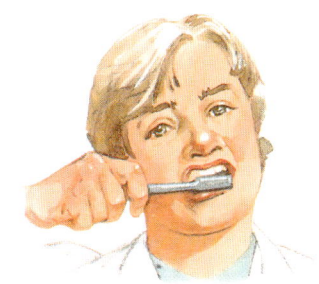

Even organisms that normally live harmlessly on or in the body can cause disease if they get into the wrong place. This is why it is so important to wash your hands carefully after using the toilet, to remove all traces of bacteria that normally live harmlessly in the lower part of the digestive system. If bacteria are transferred to the food you eat, they can cause stomach upsets and **diarrhea**.

Washing the hands before a meal is just as important, because it removes other organisms you may have picked up from the environment. Dirty fingernails can also hide organisms which could be transferred to your food.

Body odor is caused by bacteria working on the natural secretions from the skin. Wool and cotton absorb these secretions and let perspiration evaporate, but artificial fibers like nylon, rayon and acrylic are not so absorbent. Clothes made from these materials make you feel hot and sticky, and they encourage body odor. Frequent washing and daily changes of underwear will help prevent this.

Minor infections

Your skin helps to protect you from the disease organisms all around you. But if the skin is damaged by cuts or scratches, germs can enter and cause infection. Fortunately, most of these infections are irritating rather than serious.

Spots and pimples often affect young people in their teens. These result partly from changes in the chemistry of your body as you grow up, but they are made worse by the presence of bacteria on the skin.

Oily liquid is produced from the follicle at the base of each hair where it emerges from the skin. In young people, large amounts of this oily material are produced. Sometimes it forms a plug at the mouth of the follicle and darkens to produce a blackhead. Because the follicle is blocked, the trapped material causes a swelling or pimple. If it is then infected by bacteria, it becomes red and inflamed, causing **acne**.

Frequent washing helps to prevent blackheads and acne by removing this oily material and by reducing the number of bacteria present. Mild antiseptics and medicated soaps may also help to keep the skin clean.

Cold sores, caused by a virus called **herpes**, are small blisters which can develop into painful ulcers, usually at the corners of the lips or just inside the mouth. They are generally slow to heal, and often appear in groups when you are feeling run-down or suffering from an illness.

Ringworm is caused by a fungus which attacks the skin, spreading to form red, itchy circular patches. It can be caught from dogs, cats, horses or cattle, or from another infected person. Different types of ringworm affect the scalp, groin and armpits.

Boils, caused by staphylococci, are painful inflamed swellings containing pus. This material is the remains of dead cells and bacteria and sometimes needs to be removed to help healing of the boil.

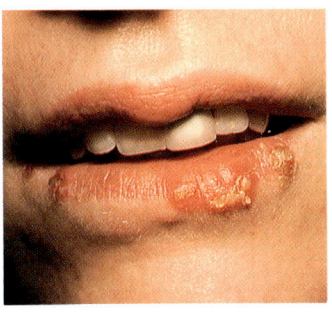
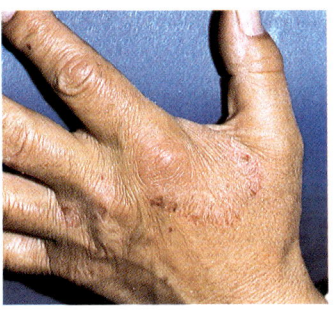
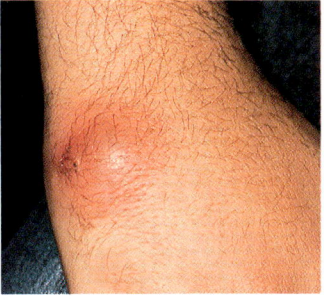

Warts are small swellings on the skin, caused by infection with a virus which makes the surrounding skin cells grow more quickly. Although warts are unsightly, they are seldom painful and often clear up without treatment.

Athlete's foot is caused by a fungus similar to ringworm, but affects only the feet. It attacks the skin between the toes. The infection is easily spread in the damp conditions of swimming pools and shower rooms, so avoid walking barefoot in such places.

Conjunctivitis or "pink eye" is an inflammation of the transparent coating of the eye, the conjunctiva. It is usually caused by viruses or bacteria, and it makes the eye pink and painful. The infection usually clears up quickly, but may need medical treatment.

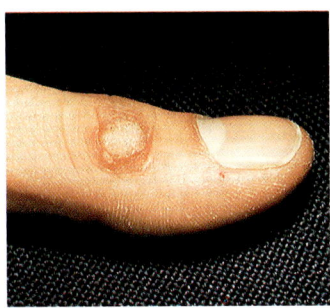
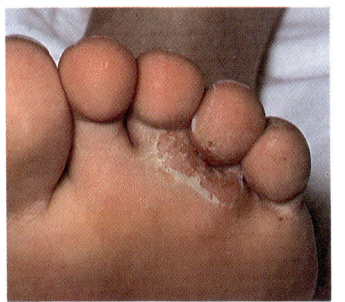
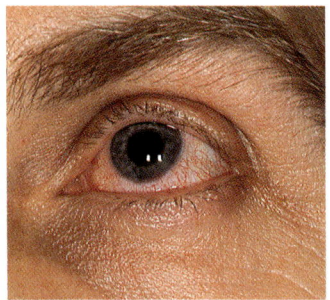

Parasite diseases

Not all the organisms that cause disease are microscopic bacteria and viruses. Other larger creatures, called **parasites**, sometimes make a home on or in our bodies. Fleas, for example, feed on the blood of humans, dogs and cats. Human fleas are now very rare, but people often get bitten by cat or dog fleas, which cause itchy spots.

Lice are tiny insect-like creatures which can live on the body's surface, clinging to the base of a hair. They feed on blood and their bites cause itching. Their large egg sacs, called "nits," stick to hairs, and the infection is easily spread when children play together, especially if they share combs or hairbrushes.

Scabies is caused by tiny mites which burrow along the outer layer of the skin. They make winding inflamed tracks which itch fiercely and can become infected by bacteria.

Various worms can sometimes infect the digestive system. Some are very tiny and cause little harm, being passed from child to child by poor toilet hygiene. Tapeworms are very large, and cause digestive upsets. They can be caught by eating types of undercooked meat.

 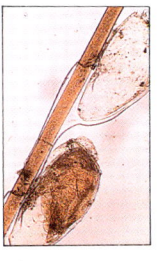   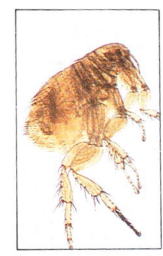 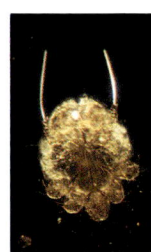

head louse   nits   tapeworm   roundworms   flea   scabies mite

Lice live on the hair of the head or body. Their bites cause itching.

Nits are the egg sacs of lice. They cling to the base of the hair.

Fleas are found on the skin where they feed by sucking blood.

Roundworms, like pinworms and threadworms, live in the gut and can cause itching around the anus.

Tapeworms are long flat parasites which live in the bowel. They are uncommon in Western countries.

Scabies is caused by tiny burrowing mites which make itchy winding tracks beneath the skin.

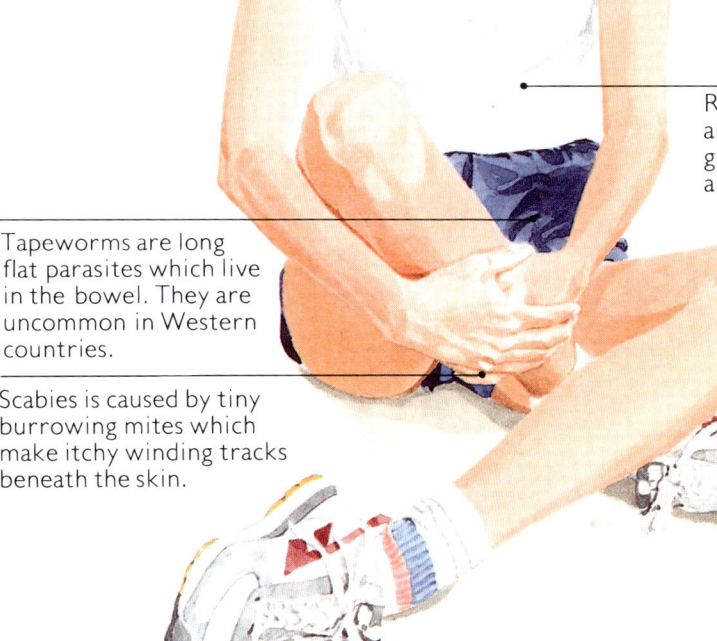

Food hygiene

Bacteria can live on almost any organic material, but food provides the ideal conditions in which they can thrive. Bacteria can "spoil" food, making it smell or taste bad, but they can also produce toxins, which have no smell or taste and which can cause food poisoning.

Foods that are bought ready-prepared are often treated to remove or kill bacteria. Canned foods are pre-cooked in the sealed can, killing any bacteria present. Many foods can be deep-frozen and kept for a long time, because the cold temperature prevents bacterial growth. But as soon as the food is thawed, the bacteria will start to grow again. That is why it is important to use thawed food quickly. You should never refreeze it, as this simply preserves the bacteria that grew while the food was thawing.

Bacteria are naturally present in some types of meat such as chicken, so it is important to cook them thoroughly. It is also important not to allow uncooked meat to be stored near cooked meat, because bacteria could easily be spread from one to the other.

Most forms of food contamination happen within the home. Cooking utensils, chopping boards and can openers often carry enormous numbers of bacteria unless they are thoroughly washed in hot soapy water, rinsed and dried after use. Bacteria also collect around drains and garbage cans in the kitchen, and flies can carry the infection to uncovered food.

Aids to kitchen hygiene in this kitchen are:
1 Covered garbage can in cupboard to keep flies out
2 Paper towels for mopping up spills
3 Easily cleaned seal between work surfaces and wall
4 Soap and towel for washing hands
5 First-aid box with antiseptic
6 Sealed storage jars
7 Plastic floor covering, easy to keep clean
8 Refrigerator for cool food storage
9 No gaps beneath furniture for pests to hide
10 Wall can opener is detachable for easy cleaning

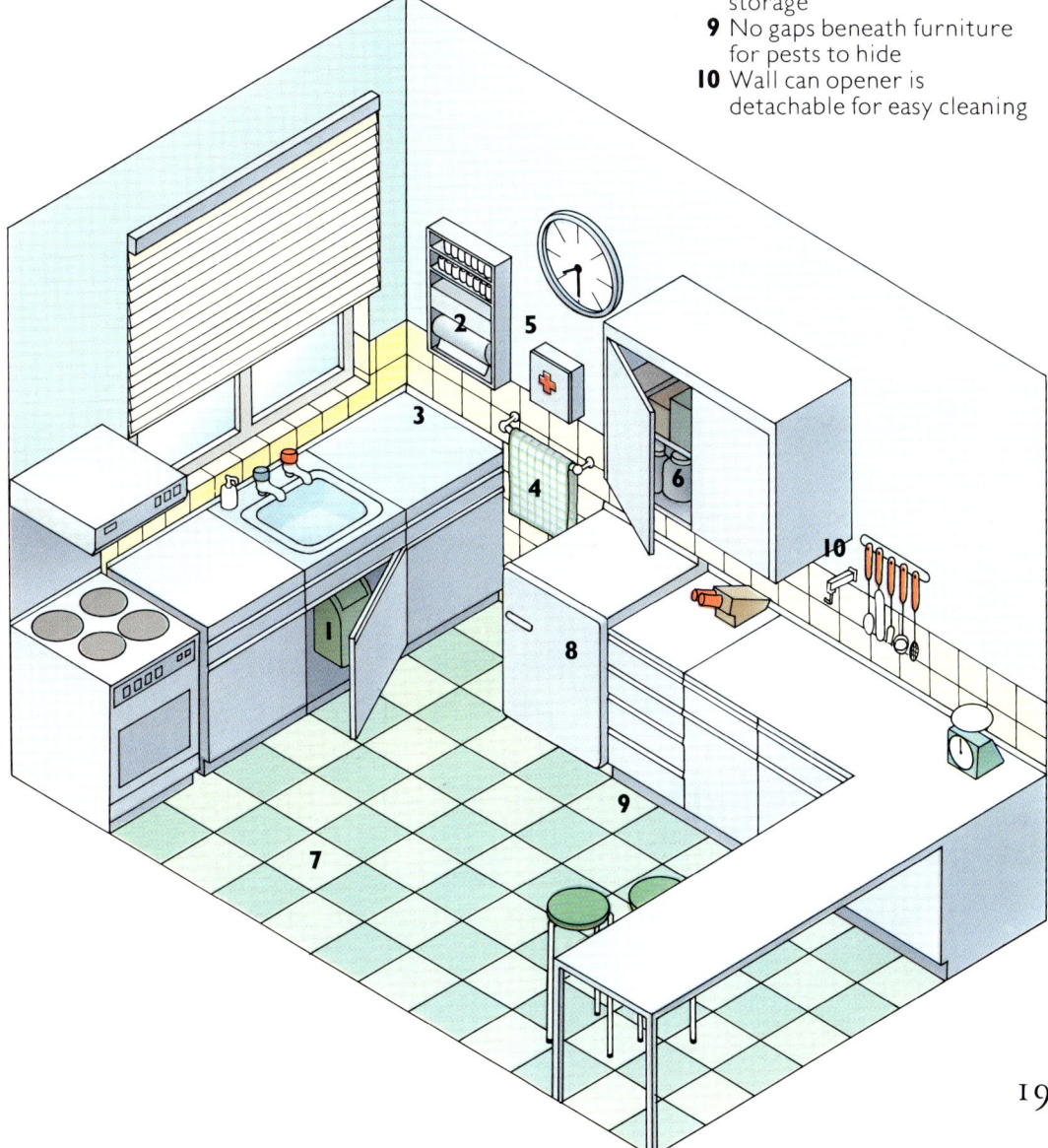

Pests that spread disease

The most common pest that spreads disease is the housefly. The fly is one of the main causes of food poisoning because of its habit of feeding on dead and decaying matter. It feeds by spreading digestive fluid on decaying matter, then sucking it back in before flying off to find a new food source. The bristly legs of the fly become coated with bacteria, which are deposited on any uncovered food on which it lands.

In warm, damp conditions cockroaches flourish. These large insects are common in warm climates, but are also found in restaurants and hospitals, where the warmth and moisture suit them. They emerge at night to scavenge and feed on food scraps, spreading bacteria over uncovered food and causing food poisoning.

Rats are also disease carriers, and are found almost everywhere in the world. They have become used to living near humans and have proved almost impossible to eradicate. Rats are known to be carriers of bubonic plague, transmitted by rat fleas to humans, although the disease now exists only in the Third World.

△ Flies feed on decaying matter, and their mouth parts and feet are heavily contaminated with bacteria. Flies are often responsible for food poisoning, causing stomach upsets and diarrhea, as well as more serious diseases.

△ Because of their habit of living and feeding among rubbish laden with germs, rats are a threat to health. Rats will also feed on and contaminate stored food such as grain.

◁ Wild animals such as foxes can be carriers of rabies.

▷ Rabies is a virus disease of the nervous system which is spread by the bite of an infected animal. Humans are usually infected by dog bites, but the disease is mostly found in wild animals such as foxes. A rabid fox may bite domestic animals such as dogs or cats, and they in turn may pass on the infection to people. Britain is free of this very dangerous disease because imported animals are put into quarantine. In the United States pets are usually vaccinated.

The spread of the rabies virus

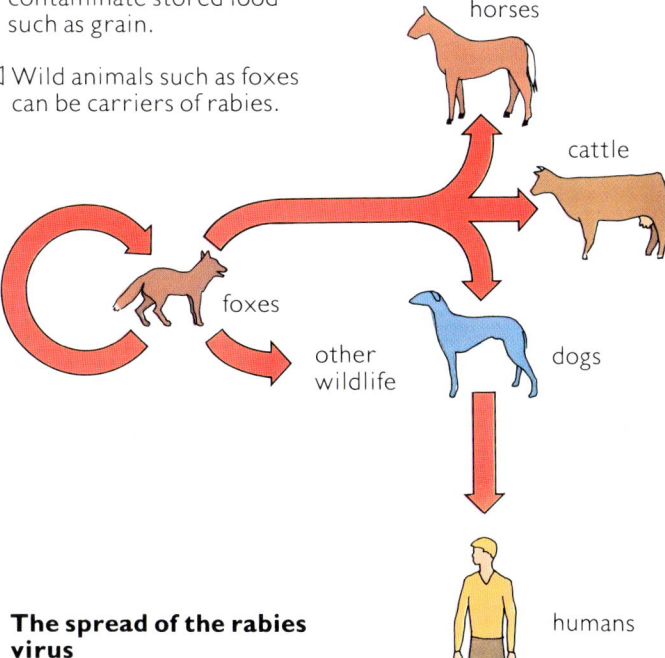

21

Vacation precautions

People who travel abroad for their vacations often pick up minor infections such as stomach upsets or diarrhea. Mostly these clear up after a few days without any special treatment.

Bacteria living naturally inside your digestive system do not normally cause problems because you have adjusted to them. But if you travel to another country, you may pick up a local variety from contaminated food or water and get various sorts of minor illness. These soon clear up as you become immune to those particular organisms.

Most people travel to warmer climates for their vacations, where bacteria breed much faster, and standards of hygiene and sewage disposal may not be as high as those you are used to. Stomach upsets can be made worse by eating rich or unfamiliar types of food.

It is important to be especially careful about everyday hygiene in warm parts of the world, and it is essential to have all the vaccinations recommended by your doctor to help protect you against serious infectious diseases such as typhoid and cholera.

Stomach upsets are common when vacationing in hot climates. Bacteria breed very rapidly in the warm conditions, and food may be contaminated. Water is often the cause of problems, so it may be wise to avoid drinking tap water or having ice in drinks. Ice cream is another common cause of diarrhea.

Coughs and sneezes

Coughs, colds and **influenza** (or "flu") are generally caused by viruses. Some people always seem to be suffering from a cold. The reason for this is that there are actually more than 100 different types of virus, each of which can cause a similar illness. As soon as we get over one type of infection, and become immune to the virus, we can then catch another, to which we have no resistance.

The symptoms of a cold are much the same, whatever the virus. The lungs, lining of the nose, throat, larynx

Influenza epidemics often seem to start in Southeast Asia. It is thought that the virus may "hide" in livestock such as pigs and ducks before emerging in a new form. At one time the disease spread gradually, carried overland and by sea, but modern jet travel means that a new strain can spread worldwide within a few days.

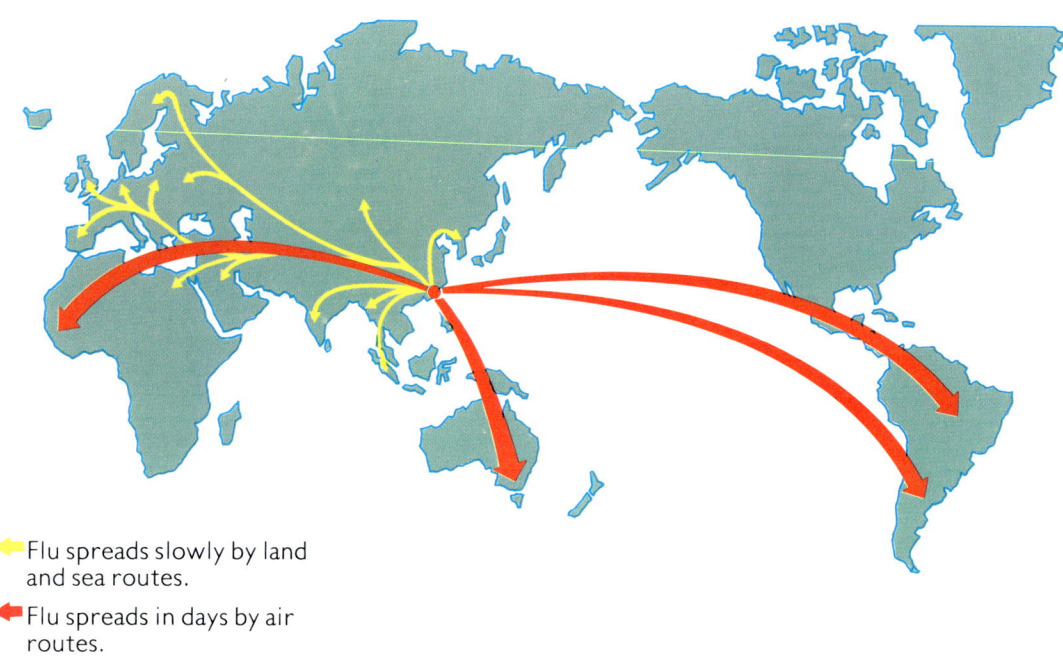

◄ Flu spreads slowly by land and sea routes.

◄ Flu spreads in days by air routes.

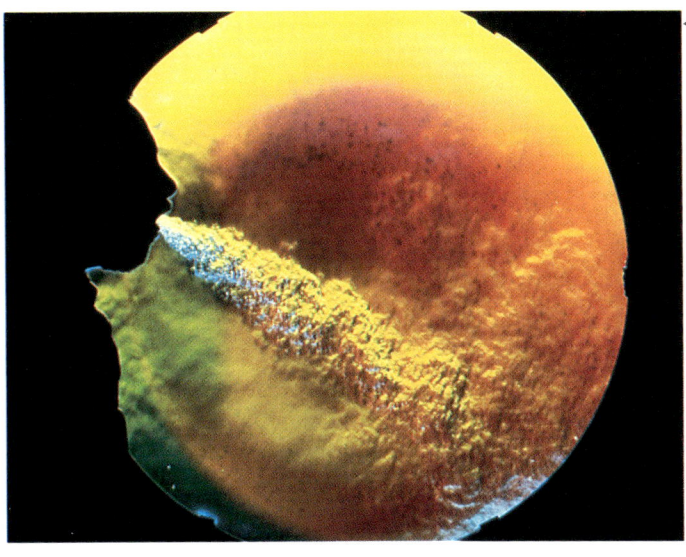

◁ When we cough, a swirling mass of air currents is produced, laden with water droplets containing viruses from the lungs. These can be inhaled by other people, spreading colds or flu.

▽ Every few years a new strain of flu virus appears, causing serious epidemics. Some reappear years later, while others apparently disappear, like the HSW virus which killed millions of people around the world in 1918.

(voicebox) or windpipe may all be affected, but different viruses may irritate one more than another.

Influenza is also caused by a virus, and at first resembles a cold. However, its symptoms are much worse and last longer, because the virus enters the bloodstream and causes a fever. There are several types of flu virus, and different **strains** usually reappear every few years, causing an **epidemic** and spreading very quickly. The flu virus changes slightly every time it reappears, so people who were immune after having the disease can still catch the new strain.

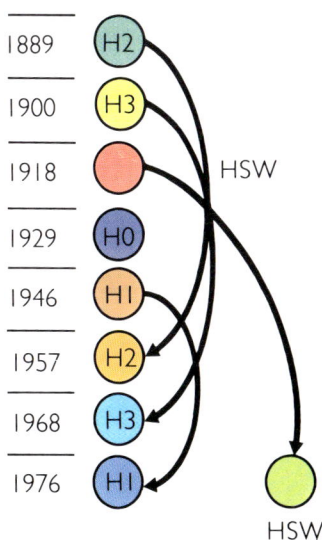

Sore throats

The throat is at risk from many different types of infection. Most "sore throats," or acute pharyngitis, are caused by viruses and last only a few days.

Tonsillitis is a very common illness which usually affects young people. The tonsils are two small glandular areas at the sides of the throat, which trap and help destroy invading microscopic organisms. Sometimes these invaders are not destroyed, but multiply in the tonsils, causing them to become red and swollen. Tonsillitis is usually caused by bacteria, and can be treated with drugs called **antibiotics**. It was once fashionable to remove the tonsils surgically to prevent

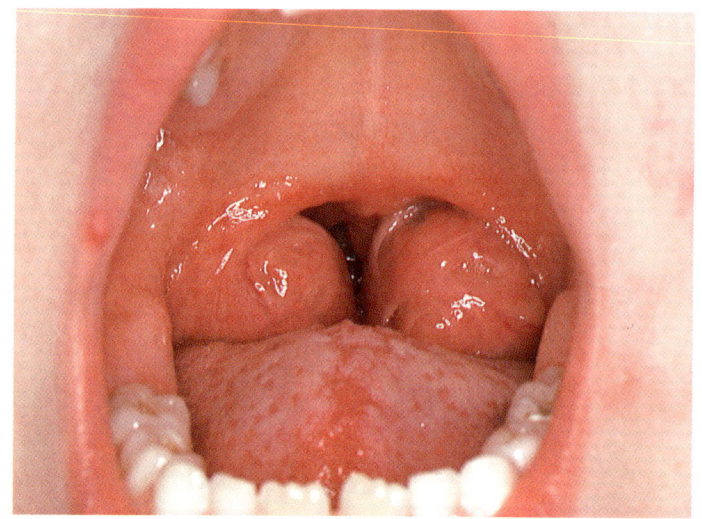

Tonsils are small patches of tissue at the sides of the throat. Normally they help to protect against infection, but when invaded by bacteria or viruses the tonsils become swollen and inflamed.

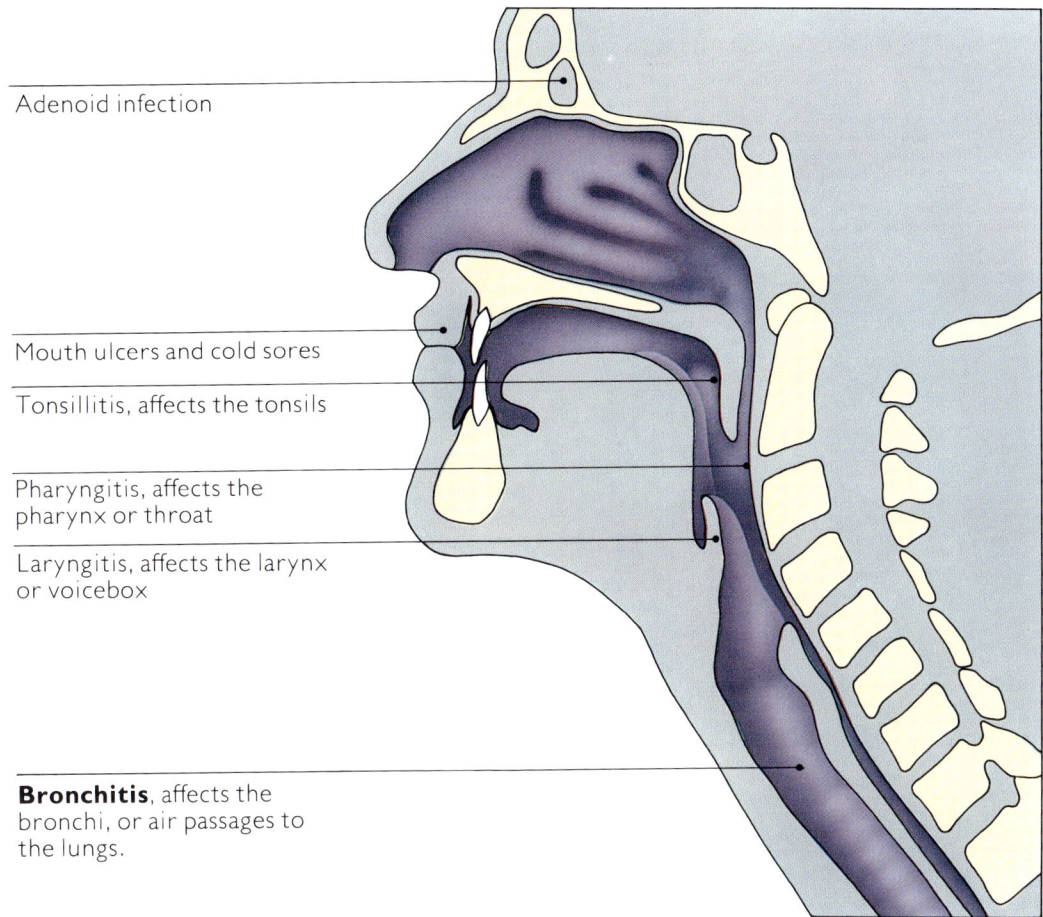

Adenoid infection

Mouth ulcers and cold sores

Tonsillitis, affects the tonsils

Pharyngitis, affects the pharynx or throat

Laryngitis, affects the larynx or voicebox

Bronchitis, affects the bronchi, or air passages to the lungs.

the infection, but this operation is not so common now. Laryngitis is an infection farther down the throat.

Other diseases that can affect the throat include **diphtheria**. This causes a skin-like film to grow across the throat, restricting breathing. Thanks to vaccination, it is now rare in developed countries. **Whooping cough** causes the breathing passages to become extremely irritated and blocked by thick mucus. However, the risk can be avoided almost completely by vaccination at an early age.

Because the mouth and throat are among the first parts of the body encountered by invading bacteria or viruses, infections in these areas are quite common. Almost any part of the mouth and throat can be infected. Although the organisms causing infection are often the same, such infections are named after the part of the mouth or throat affected.

Measles and rubella

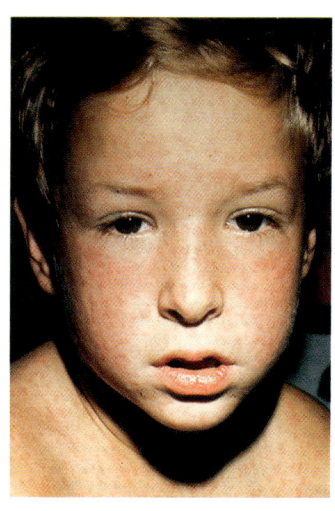

Like many infections, measles produces a rash. The doctor can usually tell what the infection is by examining the rash and taking the patient's temperature.

Measles and **rubella** (or German measles) are typical diseases of childhood, and do not usually cause serious illness in developed countries.

Rubella is usually a very mild illness – so mild that people may not even realize it was anything more than a cold. Usually the glands in the side of the neck are slightly swollen and a pink rash, starting on the face, spreads down on to the trunk. It is a virus disease, and is highly contagious. It clears up without any treatment, but the main danger is that an infected person can easily spread the virus to a pregnant woman. If a pregnant woman who has never had rubella catches the disease, the virus may attack her unborn child and cause birth defects. Deafness is particularly common in these children.

Measles is similar to rubella, but it may be much more serious. In healthy young people it seldom causes problems, but for undernourished people in the Third World, measles can be a killer. A protective vaccination is available, and this has made measles much less common in the United States.

It is important that all adolescent girls are tested to see whether they have had rubella and are properly immune. If not, they can be vaccinated to prevent them catching the disease later during pregnancy.

The importance of protection against common childhood diseases is explained by the simple leaflets available from doctors and clinics. A simple injection can save a child and its parents the misery of a long, drawn-out illness.

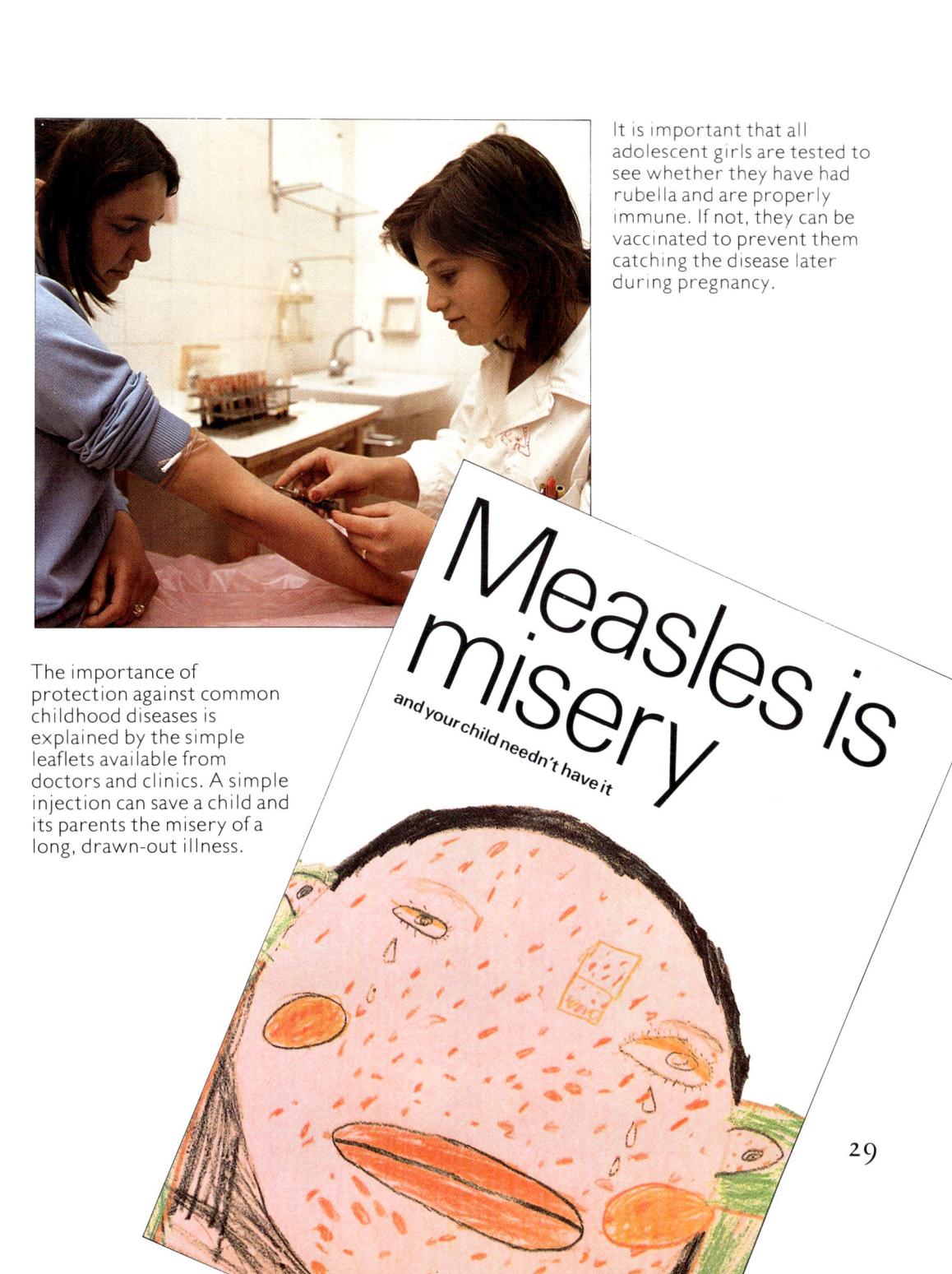

Measles is misery

and your child needn't have it

Chickenpox and mumps

Chickenpox and **mumps** are both diseases which are a nuisance in children, but can be very unpleasant for adults. Both are highly contagious.

Chickenpox is unmistakable. It produces a rash of blister-like spots, which burst and turn into dark scabs. The spots are mostly on the face, but can be scattered over the whole body. People who have chickenpox feel tired and listless and have a slight fever.

There is no real treatment for chickenpox, as it clears up quickly, and it is not possible to catch it again.

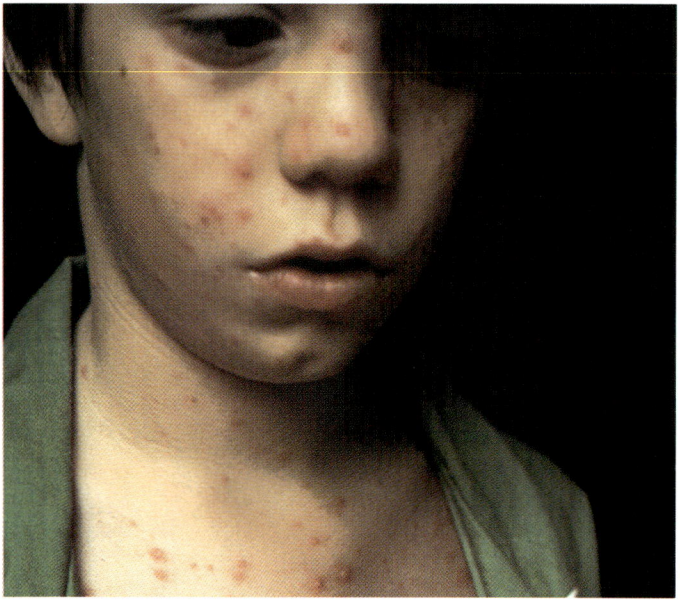

Chickenpox, caused by a virus, first produces blistery spots, which gradually turn into dark itchy scabs. It is important not to scratch these spots, as this could cause scarring. Chickenpox is not a serious disease in children, but it can make adults very ill.

Mumps (or parotitis) is caused by a virus which affects the salivary glands in the cheeks and under the chin, making them swollen and tender. The parotid glands, just in front of the ear, are usually affected first. Sometimes the infection is only on one side of the face. Swallowing can be painful and there is a fever for a few days.

Usually, there are no aftereffects, but for older boys and men the disease can be more serious, because it can attack the testes causing considerable pain and fever.

There is little doubt about the diagnosis when someone has mumps, because the sides of the face (and sometimes under the chin) become swollen and tender. Mumps is caused by a virus, and although it is uncomfortable, it does not usually make the infected person feel ill for very long.

The common infections

Disease	Spread	Incubation
Chickenpox	Virus Infectious Spread by coughs, sneezes and direct contact	2–3 weeks
Common cold	Virus Infectious Spread by coughs and sneezes	3 days
Diphtheria	Bacterium Infectious Spread by coughs, sneezes and contact with infected saliva	2–5 days
Food poisoning	Bacterium or virus Spread by contaminated food or water	Few hours
Influenza	Virus Infectious Spread by coughs and sneezes	2–3 days
Infectious hepatitis (type A)	Virus Infectious Contaminated food or water	2–6 weeks
Measles	Virus Infectious Spread by coughs and sneezes	10–14 days
Mumps	Virus Infectious Spread by droplets of infected saliva	2–3 weeks
Polio	Virus Infectious Water-borne	10–15 days
Rubella	Virus Infectious Spread by coughs and sneezes	2–3 weeks
Scarlet fever	Bacterium Infectious Spread by coughs, sneezes and direct contact	2–4 days
Tuberculosis	Bacterium Infectious Spread by infected saliva and infected milk	Very long period
Whooping cough	Bacterium Infectious Spread by coughs and sneezes	1–2 weeks
AIDS	Virus Infectious Spread by body fluids and sexual activity	May be several years. Some infected people may not develop the disease.

Period of illness	Immunity	General features
5–10 days. May be longer in adults.	Yes	Rash followed by watery spots. These burst and form dark, itchy scabs. May be slight fever.
Up to 1 week	Incomplete	Runny nose, sore throat, cough. Varies depending on type of virus involved.
Up to 2 weeks. Much longer if there are complications	Yes	High temperature, swollen glands and membrane in throat which makes breathing difficult. Complications may affect heart and nervous system.
Usually 1–2 days but may be longer	No	Vomiting and diarrhea
1 week, plus 1–2 weeks for full recovery	Yes	Chills and fever, aching joints, hacking cough and chest pains. Weakness for some time afterwards.
3–4 weeks, sometimes longer	Yes	At first resembles influenza. Pain in abdomen. Yellow skin discoloration (jaundice). Weakness for some weeks after recovery.
1 week	Yes	High temperature, cough, rash starting behind the ears and spreading down the head and trunk.
1 week	Yes	Raised temperature, swollen glands at side of face and below chin.
Varies	Yes	Headache, sore throat and fever, followed by pain in neck and back. Can cause permanent nerve damage.
3–5 days	Yes	Slight temperature, swollen glands behind ears, pale pink rash on face and body.
Up to 3 weeks	No	High temperature, sore throat. Bright red rash around mouth spreads over body.
Several months unless treated	Yes	Slight fever, weight loss; symptoms depend on part of body affected. Usually attacks lungs first.
2–10 weeks or more	Yes	Early symptoms like a feverish cold. Then severe coughing fits with a characteristic whooping noise.
Up to 2 years	No	Weakness, weight loss, failure of immune system. AIDS sufferers are affected by other diseases or by tumours. Once the disease develops it is apparently always fatal.

Fighting disease

When disease organisms attack the body, we can be affected in a number of different ways. First, the organisms must enter the body in large numbers. For a while, there is no obvious effect. This is called the **incubation** period, while the organism is becoming established. Sometimes the organisms are restricted to a small area, as happens with "local" infections. In "general" infections, the organisms enter the bloodstream and spread throughout the body.

The most obvious signs of the battle taking place inside us are high temperature or fever, plus reddening or inflammation of the affected part of the body. Although the fever and inflammation are uncomfortable, they are signs that the body is fighting the disease.

Our **immune system** fights the disease organisms by releasing special chemicals into the blood and surrounding tissues. At this stage, you may feel quite ill, because of all the substances being released into your body. As you begin to recover, you feel run-down and weak. Sometimes the recovery period is very long, as in **glandular fever**.

1 It may be several days before you discover that you have caught an infection from someone else. The first signs are usually sneezing, a sore throat or a cough.

2 As the infection takes hold, the organisms reproduce in huge numbers and the body begins to fight back. It reacts against the organisms and the substances they produce, and this causes inflammation and a fever. Because you sweat a lot when you have a fever, you will need to drink plenty of water to replace your body fluids.

3 When your body begins to win its fight against the invading organisms, your system will be full of chemical substances that have been used to attack the germs. It will also contain large numbers of dead or dying viruses or bacteria and the substances they have produced. The body needs to repair itself, so it is a natural reaction to sleep, using as little energy as possible, and not putting further strain on the system.

4 After a serious infection, you may feel weak and listless for quite a long time as the repair process continues. You must gradually build up your strength, eating properly and getting plenty of rest.

Developing immunity against disease

We have several natural defenses against infection. Tears, for example, contain chemicals which can destroy bacteria. And the stomach juices quickly kill most organisms entering through the mouth.

Once inside the body, disease organisms are attacked by the immune system. Living disease organisms and the substances they release into the blood carry chemicals which can be recognized by the body as being "foreign." These are known as **antigens**, and they trigger the body's defenses.

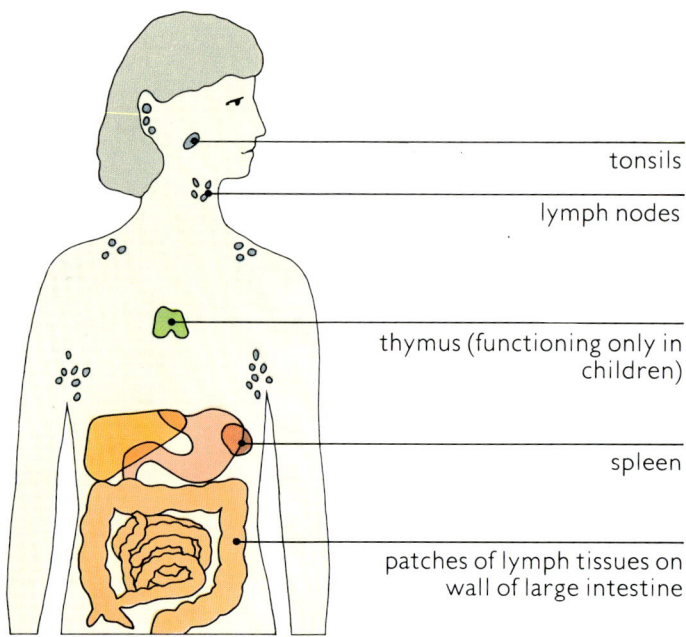

The immune system is spread out through the body. Cells which attack invading organisms are produced or stored until they are needed. Some of the glands or lymph nodes associated with the immune system swell up as they fight infection and can be felt under the skin as small lumps.

tonsils

lymph nodes

thymus (functioning only in children)

spleen

patches of lymph tissues on wall of large intestine

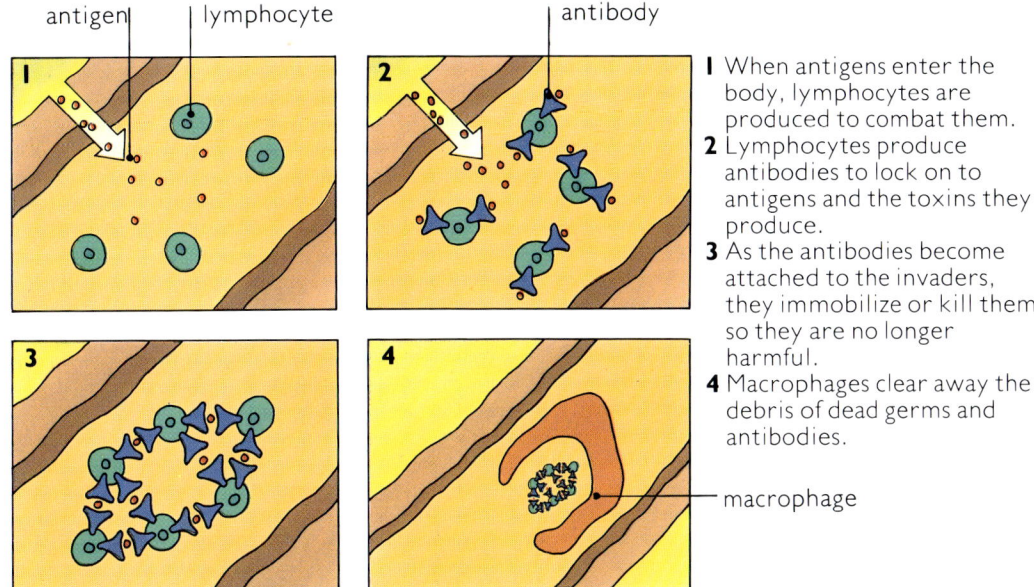

1. When antigens enter the body, lymphocytes are produced to combat them.
2. Lymphocytes produce antibodies to lock on to antigens and the toxins they produce.
3. As the antibodies become attached to the invaders, they immobilize or kill them, so they are no longer harmful.
4. Macrophages clear away the debris of dead germs and antibodies.

There are special white blood cells in the body called **lymphocytes**, which produce **antibodies**. These are substances which fit on to antigens as a key fits a lock. For each antigen there is a special antibody. Once the body has made the proper antibody to fit an antigen it has never encountered before, it can "remember" how to do this for a long while.

As the antibodies lock on to the antigens, they gradually block the release of dangerous chemicals produced by the antigens. The chemicals, called toxins, cause many of the symptons of disease. The antibodies eventually cause the antigens to clump together in harmless groups, where they can be consumed by large wandering cells called **macrophages**. These swarm into the area of infection, clearing up dead cells and debris.

Protection against disease

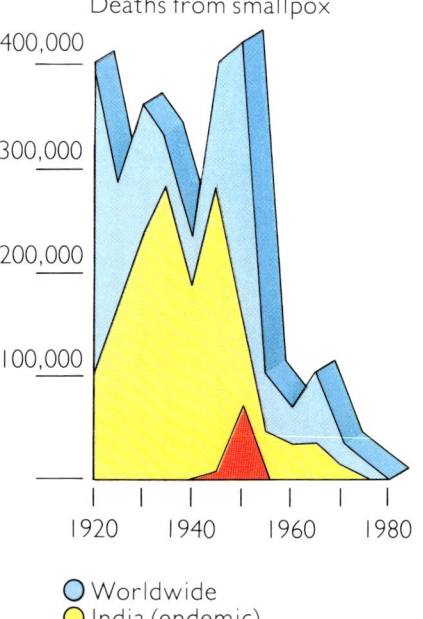

The disease smallpox has been successfully eradicated through vaccination. In China there were brief epidemics, the last in the 1950s. In India the disease was endemic (present all the time) until it was finally wiped out in the 1970s.

Deaths from smallpox

○ Worldwide
○ India (endemic)
● China (epidemic)

Although one way to become immune to a disease is to catch it, a much easier way is to be "given" it in a carefully controlled form. To protect against serious illnesses such as **polio** or TB, a very mild strain of the organism can be given which does not cause the disease, but which persuades the body to defend itself and produce antibodies. Sometimes the organisms are specially treated to weaken them, or are killed before being injected into the body. Vaccinations of this sort can be given by injection or by scratching the skin or, occasionally, by mouth.

In an emergency, when a person is very weak, or is known to have been exposed to a dangerous disease, an extract from the blood of a person who has recovered from that disease can be given. This already contains antibodies, so it provides immediate protection, although this lasts for only a short time.

Immunity may be for life, or can be quite brief. Sometimes, as in the case of flu, the disease organism may change its structure, and it is no longer recognized by the immune system. We are once more susceptible to its effects.

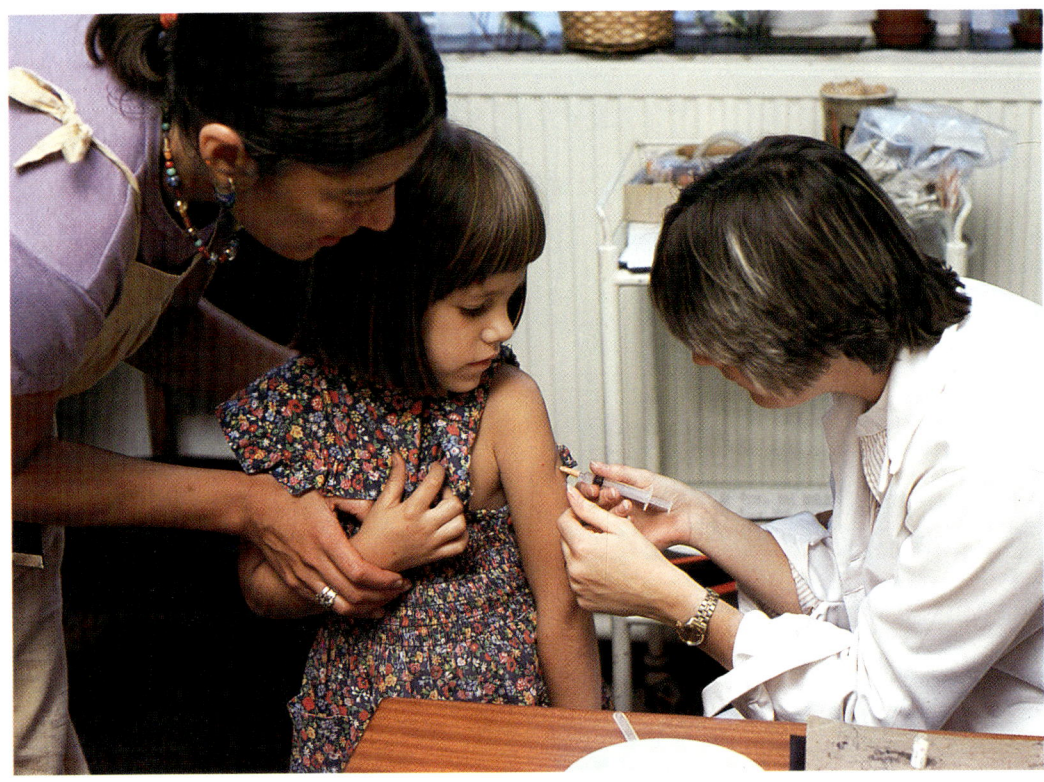

△ Vaccinations against potentially serious diseases are now given to most children, and this practice has helped to make many diseases much less common. Often the vaccination is given by injection, or by scratching the skin, allowing weakened or harmless organisms to enter the body and cause the reaction which will lead to immunity.

▷ For diseases such as polio, vaccination with a weakened strain of the disease is given by mouth, usually as drops placed on a sugar lump. This means that large numbers of children can be vaccinated with the minimum of fuss, and without the need for sterile needles.

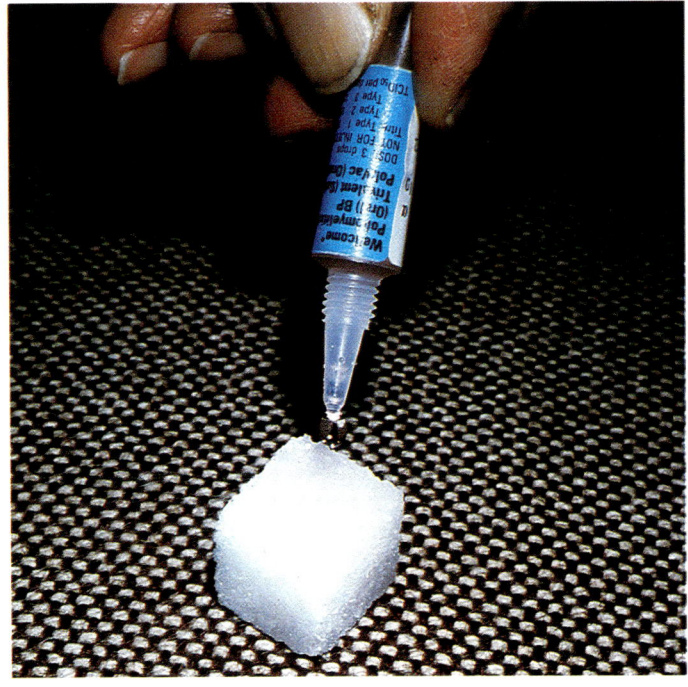

Fighting disease with drugs

Both bacteria and viruses can often be controlled by vaccination, but unlike most viruses, bacteria can also be controlled by drugs called antibiotics.

A bacterium has a tough cell wall, which splits when it reproduces to make two new cells. Some antibiotics interfere with the formation of a new cell wall, so the bacterium either dies or is defenseless against the body's immune system. Other antibiotics prevent the bacterium from reproducing, so it dies off naturally.

Antibiotics are a group of drugs, some of which occur naturally. The first to be discovered was penicillin, which was extracted from a mold like that which grows on stale bread.

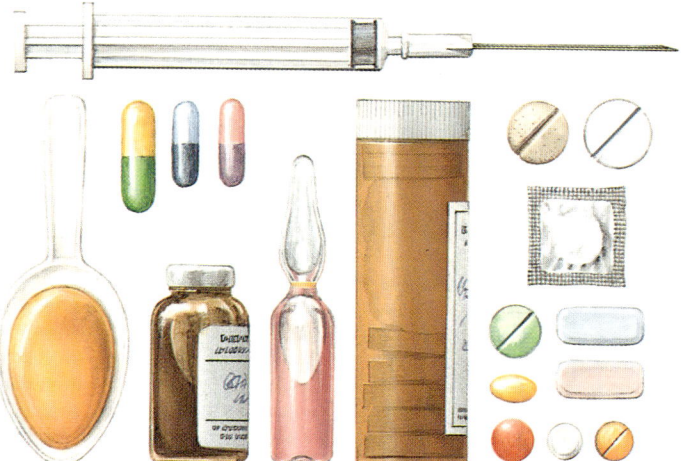

Modern drugs can be taken in a variety of different ways — sometimes to make them more effective, and sometimes because patients prefer certain types of tablets, drops or creams. Some modern antibiotic drugs kill most types of bacteria, while others attack only a few of the most dangerous types. The doctor must decide which organism is causing the problem before prescribing a drug.

In many parts of the world, people prefer to rely on their traditional medicines. Some of the medicines in this Chinese pharmacy may seem strange to us, but many of these traditional remedies have been found to contain powerful drugs.

Most antibiotics are now made chemically, rather than by growing the organisms that produce them.

There are many different types of bacteria, and no antibiotic is effective against all of them. Sometimes the doctor has to try several different types before the disease is controlled. Like viruses, bacteria can change to avoid the body's defenses or a particular antibiotic. The bacteria then multiply freely.

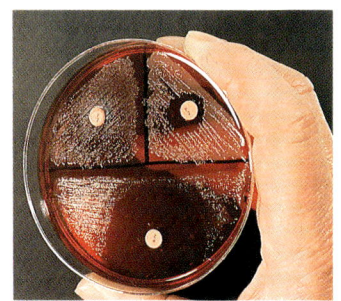

Antibiotic drugs are tested on bacteria grown in dishes. Colonies of bacteria can be seen as small shiny patches. The antibiotic has stopped their growth in some areas.

Tropical diseases

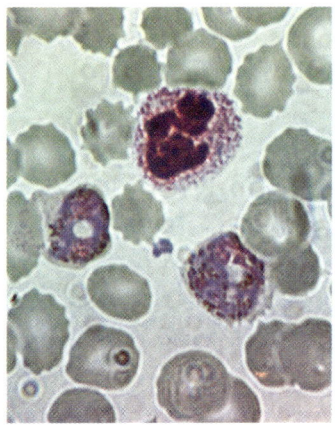

Some of the most serious infections affect people who already suffer from malnutrition and poor hygiene in the tropical parts of the world. People weakened by starvation or a poor diet are much more susceptible to the effects of infection.

Many of the most serious diseases of the tropics are caused by organisms that have a complicated life cycle.

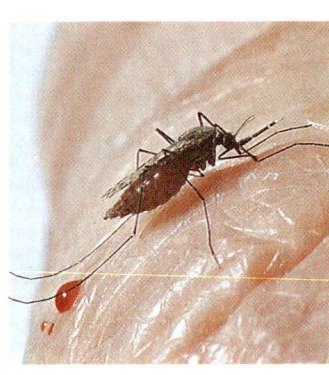

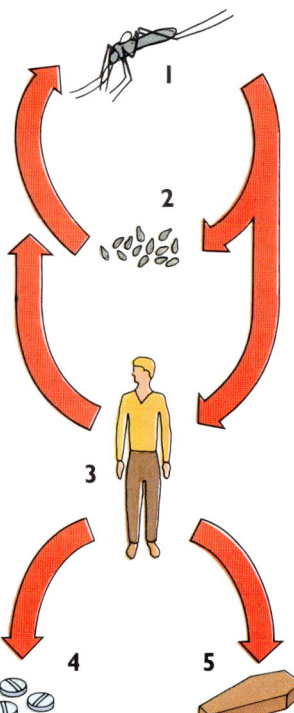

△ The anopheles mosquito (*above*) feeds on human blood. As it feeds, it injects saliva, which may be infected with the malaria parasite. The parasite then attacks the red blood cells (*top*). It is important to be protected against mosquito bites in areas where malaria occurs.

1 Malaria is spread by the anopheles mosquito. Malaria parasites reproduce inside the mosquito and collect in its salivary glands.
2 Mosquitoes lay their eggs in stagnant water. Draining swampy areas destroys the habitat of the larvae and cuts the life cycle of the parasite.
3 When the mosquito bites a human, the malaria parasites are injected into the blood where they damage blood cells. When another mosquito feeds on the blood, it takes in the parasite and spreads the disease.
4 Certain drugs can provide protection against malaria and control the disease.
5 If untreated, malaria can cause long illness leading to death.

△ The parasite that causes bilharziasis lives in contaminated water. It can burrow through unprotected skin. Once inside the body, it develops into worm-like larvae.

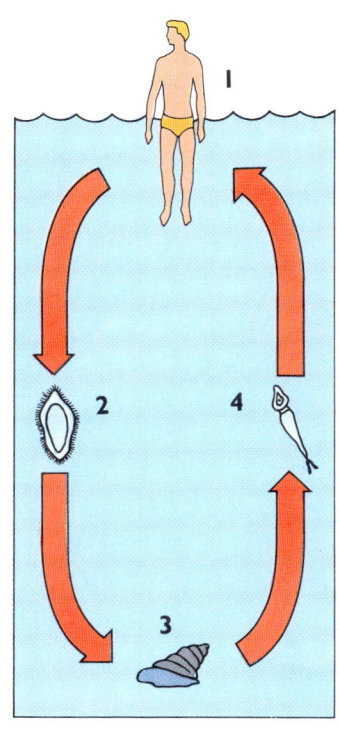

Bilharziasis affects millions of people in the tropics.

1. Infected people spread the disease when they urinate into water, passing out the eggs of the parasite.
2. The parasite eggs hatch, and the emerging larvae swim off in search of a particular type of water snail.
3. The parasites burrow into the snail and multiply.
4. Parasites emerge and swim in search of people wading or swimming in the river. They burrow into the skin and attack the bladder and other organs.

These organisms do not spread directly from one person to another, but are often carried by biting insects. Many of these organisms spend parts of their lives in other animals, and this can make them difficult to control. **Yellow fever**, for example, affects humans and monkeys, and the disease is spread from one to the other by biting mosquitoes.

Because diseases such as yellow fever and **malaria** are spread by mosquito bites, it is possible to prevent them by destroying the insects.

Contaminated water is the source of many tropical diseases. The disease organisms thrive in the hot climate and infect people drinking the water or wading in it.

AIDS: a new threat to health

AIDS is a dangerous disease which has only recently appeared. It is caused by a virus, but signs of the disease may not appear until several years after a person is infected. The AIDS virus attacks the lymphocytes, the white blood cells which are such an essential part of the immune system. As a result, the body has no defenses against infection. The AIDS virus does not cause disease itself, but because the immune system is damaged, various other organisms which are normally harmless can cause serious disease, which is fatal sooner or later.

The AIDS virus is carried in the blood and other body fluids. It can be spread from one person to another during sexual activity, or by contact with infected blood. Drug users who inject drugs with a shared needle are particularly at risk.

Not all of those who carry the AIDS virus become ill, but for those who do, the future is bleak. At present there is no real cure, although drugs are being developed to slow down the progress of the disease. The greatest challenge for scientists now is to develop a vaccine against AIDS.

In this photograph, tiny particles of AIDS virus can be seen dotted over the surface of a white blood cell. The viruses reproduce inside the cell, and destroy it when they burst out. Cells carrying the AIDS virus cannot carry out their normal function of protecting the body from infection, so AIDS patients have no immunity to disease.

As yet, there is no effective treatment for AIDS, so the only realistic way to control the spread of AIDS is to persuade people to change their behavior.

Glossary

Abscess: infected swelling which becomes filled with pus

Acne: skin condition in which the roots or follicles of hairs become infected, causing inflamed spots, usually on the face.

AIDS: virus disease which attacks the immune system. It is spread by contact with infected blood, or by sexual activity with an infected person.

Antibiotic: drug which interferes with the reproduction of bacteria, allowing them to be destroyed by the body's immune system.

Antibody: chemical substance produced by lymphocytes which immobilizes antigens so that they can be destroyed.

Antigen: a substance which is capable of causing the immune system to respond by producing defensive antibodies.

Bacteria: microscopic organisms living in almost any type of environment. Some types of bacteria cause disease when they enter the body.

Bronchitis: disease in which the bronchi, large tubes carrying air to and from the lungs, become infected and inflamed. Very common among smokers.

Chickenpox: common childhood disease caused by a virus. Chickenpox causes skin spots, followed by scabs.

Cocci: type of bacteria which are always round in shape.

Conjunctivitis ("pink eye"): inflammation of the conjunctiva, the membrane that covers the front of the eyeball.

Contagious disease: infectious disease that can be spread by contact with an infected person.

Cystitis: inflammation of the urethra, the small tube carrying urine out of the bladder. Cystitis makes urination very painful.

Diarrhea: condition where normally solid feces are passed in a liquid form. It usually occurs when infection or unfamiliar foods irritate the bowel and cause partly digested food to be passed through very quickly.

Diphtheria: throat infection caused by bacteria, which can cause closure of the throat.

Endemic: describes an infection that is always present in a population.

Epidemic: describes an infection that attacks a large number of people over a short time.

Follicle: the base or "root" of a hair.

Fungus (plural fungi): organism that normally feeds harmlessly on the skin surface, but can sometimes enter the skin and cause unpleasant rashes and itching. Fungi cause ringworm and athlete's foot.

Glandular fever (infectious mononucleosis): virus disease which commonly affects teenagers. It can be caught from infected saliva, and is often called kissing disease. Glandular fever is seldom serious, but makes sufferers feel very weak for a long time.

Hepatitis: inflammation of the liver, which may cause the skin to become yellow or jaundiced. Infectious hepatitis is caused by a virus.

Herpes: a type of virus which is responsible for mouth ulcers and cold sores.

Immune system: the mechanism which protects the body from invading organisms such as bacteria and viruses. Some illnesses are caused when the immune system incorrectly identifies a harmless substance as a dangerous invader, and reacts against it.

Incubation: the period between infection and the appearance of the first symptoms of a disease.

Infectious disease: a disease caused by micro-organisms and spread when they are passed from one person to another.

Influenza: virus disease which produces very severe cold-like sysmptoms. It causes fever, aching, sneezing and painful coughing. Influenza or flu is generally a winter disease, and frequently causes epidemics.

Lymphocyte: cell which forms an important part of the immune system, producing antibodies to fight disease. It is attacked by the AIDS virus, preventing the immune system from defending the body.

Macrophage: type of cell that clears up the debris left after an infection, consuming dead and dying bacteria and viruses, and the remains of damaged cells.

Malaria: disease caused by microscopic organisms which are injected into the body by the bite of an infected mosquito.

Measles: virus disease of children, which causes a fever and rash. It can be prevented by vaccination.

Meningitis: dangerous infection of the membranes covering the brain.

Mumps: common virus disease of children, affecting the salivary glands and causing the face and neck to become swollen.

Parasite: an organism which lives in or on its host (another organism), usually causing damage or disease. Bacteria, viruses, worms and fungi are all parasites, as well as fleas and lice living on the skin.

Plaque: layer of sticky bacteria which forms on the teeth, and is responsible for causing dental decay and eventually gum damage. It can be removed by regular cleaning of the teeth.

Pneumonia: serious lung infection caused by bacteria or viruses, leading to fever and severe shortness of breath.

Polio: virus disease carried in infected water. The polio virus lives in the gastro-intestinal tract, but when it gets into the nervous system it can cause damage which may lead to paralysis. Polio was formerly common, but can now be prevented by vaccination.

Rubella: virus disease, common in childhood. It produces a rash and a mild fever, but is not usually serious. But in pregnancy, rubella can be very dangerous for the unborn child, so vaccination is important for all girls during adolescence.

Scabies: a skin disease caused by tiny insect-like parasites which burrow beneath the skin. Scabies causes intense itching, and is contagious.

Scarlet fever: a disease caused by bacteria, which was formerly very serious. It is now unusual, and seldom causes severe illness.

Strain: a particular type of bacterium or virus which differs from others enough so that existing immunity is incomplete or absent. For example, there are several strains of influenza, which is why we can still become infected with a different strain after having had flu.

Toxin: poisonous substance produced by some types of bacteria. Toxins produce many of the effects of an infection.

Tuberculosis: bacterial disease that can affect the lungs or many other parts of the body. It was formerly common, but is now rare, due to effective vaccination.

Vaccination: method of preventing disease by giving weakened or killed viruses or bacteria, or substances extracted from them. This causes the body to produce protective antibodies which prevent infection from the actual organism.

Virus: tiny particles which, when they enter a cell, can take over its function and multiply, damaging the cell and causing disease.

Whooping cough: serious infectious disease which, by partly blocking the air passages, causes loud whooping or gasping noises as the sufferer tries to breathe. It is prevented by vaccination.

Yeast: microscopic fungus which usually lives harmlessly on the skin and in the gut. Some types of yeast can cause diseases such as thrush, which affects the mouth or sexual organs.

Yellow fever: very serious tropical virus disease spread by the bite of mosquitoes. It also affects monkeys, and this makes it difficult to eradicate.

Index

abscess 9, 46
acne 14, 46
adenoids 27
AIDS 32, 44–45, 46
antibiotics 26, 40–41
antibody 37, 38, 46
antigen 36, 37, 46
athlete's foot 15

bacteria 8, 10, 12, 13, 15, 18–19, 20, 22, 32, 35, 36, 40, 41, 46
bilharziasis 43
blackhead 14
blood plasma 38
body odor 13
boils 9, 15
bronchitis 27, 46
bubonic plague 20

chickenpox 30, 32, 46
cholera 22
cocci 9, 46
cockroaches 20
cold see common cold
cold sore 15, 27
common cold 10, 24, 32
conjunctivitis 15, 46
contagious 10
coughs 11, 25, 35
cystitis 9, 46

diarrhea 13, 21, 22, 46
diphtheria 27, 32, 46
disease 6, 8, 34–35, 40–41
drinking water 6, 22, 43
drugs, illegal 11, 44
drugs, medicinal 40–41

endemic 38, 46
epidemic 24, 25, 38, 46

fever 8, 30, 31, 34, 35
fingernails 13
fleas 16, 17, 20
flies 19, 20, 21

flu see influenza
follicle 9, 14, 46
food 18–19
food poisoning 18, 21, 32
fungi 8, 15, 46

German measles see rubella
germs 11, 14
glandular fever 34, 46

hair 16, 17
hepatitis 32, 46
herpes 15, 46

immune system 35, 38, 40, 44, 46
immunity 24, 32, 38, 39
incubation 32, 34, 46
infection 6, 10, 34, 35, 44
inflammation 8, 34, 35
influenza 10, 24, 25, 32, 46
insects 11, 20, 43

jaundice 9

laryngitis 27
lice 16, 17
liver 9
lungs 9, 25
lymphocyte 37, 46

macrophage 37, 47
malaria 42, 43, 47
malnutrition 42
measles 28, 29, 32, 42, 47
meningitis 9, 47
mites 16, 17
mosquitoes 42, 43
mouth ulcer 27
mumps 30, 31, 32, 47

nits 16, 17

parasites 16–17, 42, 47
penicillin 40
perspiration 12, 13

pharyngitis 26, 27
pimples 14
plaque 13, 47
pneumonia 9, 47
polio 32, 38, 39, 47

quarantine 21

rabies 21
rash 28
rats 20, 21
ringworm 15
rubella 28, 32, 47

scabies 16, 17, 47
scarlet fever 32, 47
skin 12, 14, 15
smallpox 6, 38
sneezes 11, 35
sore throat 9, 26–27, 35
spots 14, 30
staphylococcus 15
strain (of virus) 25, 47
stomach upsets 13, 18, 22
streptococcus 9
swollen glands 28, 31

tapeworms 16, 17
throat 26–27
tonsillitis 26, 27
toxin 8, 18, 47
tuberculosis 9, 32, 38, 47
typhoid 22

vaccination 6, 9, 22, 27, 28, 38–39, 40, 47
viruses 8, 10, 15, 24, 26, 27, 28, 30, 32, 35, 40, 44, 47

warts 15
washing 6, 13, 14
whooping cough 27, 32, 47
worms 16, 17

yeasts 8, 47
yellow fever 43, 47

48